Heather and Mike Roe

Illustrated by Betheny Lusk

gatekeeper press
Tampa, Florida

Gracie's First Day

Published by Gatekeeper Press
7853 Gunn Hwy., Suite 209
Tampa, FL 33626
www.GatekeeperPress.com

Library of Congress Control Number: 2023942586

ISBN (hardcover): 9781662937965
ISBN (paperback): 9781662937972
eISBN: 9781662937989

Dedicated to Kathy Stevens,
the most self-sacrificing mother
a man could ever have and
the force behind my passion for writing.
I love you and miss you every day.

And to Daniel, Hayden, Nick, and Andrew.
It is a privilege to watch you grow.

Special thanks to Millie Weers,
Kevin Lusk, Landon Lusk, Cheryl Dempsey,
Gina McReynolds Campbell,
and Rob Kay.

In a town nearby, in a house painted blue,
lived a little girl named Gracie and her grandmother, too.

This morning was different, in a really big way.
Gracie was going to school on her very first day.

She buttoned her coat and put on her shoes;
she grabbed her lunch box and was ready to cruise.

Gracie climbed up and buckled into the car.
They were off to the schoolhouse, which wasn't too far.

She went through the big doors and down the hall,
where Gracie saw "Kindergarten" up on the wall.

She turned and went through the door to Room 1.
Grandma gave her a kiss and said, "I love you, have fun!"

She saw children sitting on the carpet in the corner.
A woman said, "Hello, my name is Ms. Horner.

Choose a spot with the others, and in a minute or two,
you'll meet your classmates, and they will meet you."

**Gracie turned to look, but Grandma wasn't there.
She tried not to show that she was a bit scared.**

She walked over and found a spot on the floor.
She sat down and thought, *What else is in store?*

GRACIE HAD A CHOICE TO MAKE . . .
She could think about home and wonder why
Grandma had left her and sit there and cry.

**Or she could play in Ms. Horner's first game,
having fun and learning everyone's name.
WHAT WOULD YOU DO?**

She met the other students, which was so much fun.
Ms. Horner read a story, and it was a good one.

Before she knew it, they were on to the next thing.
Everyone moved to the tables for fingerpainting.

Gracie wasn't sure if she would like to do art.
But in the blink of an eye, it was time to start.

GRACIE HAD A CHOICE TO MAKE . . .
She could stand and watch what the others would do
as they all got messy, trying something new.

Or she could try it herself and you never know;
when art is over, she'd have a picture to show.

Whatever she does, it will be ok.
It's her choice; she can do it her way.
WHAT WOULD YOU DO?

They put away the paints and pictures in their drawer.
Ms. Horner said, "Please line up at the back door."

It was time to go outside on this sunny day.
Gracie couldn't wait to run and play.

They flew out the door, all wild and free.
Gracie tripped and fell and bumped her knee.

She sat up and looked around.
Her eyes teared up and she started to frown.

Then Nate ran by and tagged her arm.
He caught her off guard and she was alarmed.

He said, "You're it!" as he made a dash.
She jumped up, gave chase, and tagged him back in a flash.

Gracie smiled and yelled, "You can't catch me!"
And just like that, she forgot about her knee.

Even though her leg still hurt, just a bit,
she wasn't going to be tagged; she wasn't going to be it.

Gracie ran and played and had so much fun.
She was a little sad when recess was done.

Ms. Horner asked, "Who's hungry?"
Gracie had a hunch
that now it was time for them to eat lunch.

Ms. Horner told the class to wash their hands and face.
They were moving so fast. It felt like a race.

Gracie grabbed her lunch box and headed back to her chair.
Then she noticed someone else was sitting there.

She looked around to find another spot.
She started to get nervous; her face felt red-hot.

GRACIE HAD A CHOICE TO MAKE . . .
She could stop and worry what the others thought,
and forget about all the yummy food that she had brought.

Or she could find another seat and make a new friend.
And as luck would have it, there was a seat next to Brooke at the end.

Gracie sat down without thinking twice.
She was glad that she did because Brooke was so nice.

They ate and talked about family and toys.
They liked being at school and meeting other girls and boys.

When lunchtime was over and all the food was gone,
Ms. Horner said, "Class, clear your tables. It's time to move on."

The afternoon was filled
with things to learn.
Gracie and her new friends
were having fun taking turns.

The rest of the day went off
without a hitch.
Each station was more fun every
time she would switch.

She colored and traced letters,
dressed up as a queen,
until Ms. Horner said,
"Time to get our room clean.

Pair up and I'll give you a task."
Gracie didn't know which
friend she would ask.

She had so much fun outside with Nate,
but Brooke had made lunchtime really great.

She turned around, still not sure how she felt,
when Nate and Brooke each chose someone else.

GRACIE HAD A CHOICE TO MAKE . . .
She could let that moment take her smile away,
feel sad, and let it ruin her day.

Instead, Gracie saw Johnny standing in the back alone.
So, she made another friend before it was time to go home.

At 2:30, Ms. Horner said, "Children, get all packed up.
I'll see you tomorrow; our time today is up."

Grandma walked through the door, ready to take her away;
Gracie couldn't wait to tell her all about her day.

THE END

HIDDEN PICTURES

Each of these objects is somewhere in this book.

I'll bet you can find them!
You should go back and take a look!

GRACIE'S FIRST DAY
THE IDEA BEHIND THE STORY

Beyond Social Emotional Learning

Follow Gracie as she navigates her first day
of kindergarten to see how her response determines
whether she has a great day, or a difficult one.
Gracie could be upset when she loses her seat at lunch,
or she could use it as an opportunity to meet someone new.
Children learn that how they handle a situation emotionally
is the most important factor in their experience.
It's not what happens; it's how we respond
that really matters.

TEACHING OBJECTIVES

- **Teach resilience in the face of adversity.**

- **Guide students to recognize their emotions and overcome initial negative thoughts.**

- **Show that positive reactions can lead to unexpected benefits like new friendships.**

- **Emphasize the benefits of meeting new people.**

- **Demonstrate how stepping outside our comfort zone often leads to the most positive outcomes.**

- **Show how thoughts and focus are powerful tools in our daily lives.**

Printed in the USA
CPSIA information can be obtained
at www.ICGtesting.com
LVHW081116040124
767941LV00014B/595